YOU JUST DON'T KNOW MY STRUGGLE

PHASE II: Overcoming Addiction

Michael Burton

You just don't know my struggle:
Phase II: Overcoming Addiction. Michael Burton

Copyright © 2016 by Michael Burton
All rights reserved. This book or any portion thereof
may not be reproduced or used in any manner whatsoever
without the express written permission of the publisher
except for the use of brief quotations in a book review.

Printed in the United States of America

First Printing

ISBN 978-1-943284-08-5 (pbk.)

ISBN 978-1-943284-09-2 (ebk)

A2Z Books Publishing
1990 Young Rd
Lithonia, GA 30058

www.A2ZBooksPublishing.com

Manufactured in the United States of America

A2Z Books Publishing has allowed this work to remain exactly as the author intended, verbatim.

*My name is **Michael J. Burton** and this is **Phase II** of my life story.*
I am a recovering drug addict and I grew up in a small town called Hartwell GA. This town was so small that everyone knew one another, but it shaped me into the person I am today.

*The reason I am telling you my story is to let everyone know that **God** is real and if you put your trust in him; He will make a way out of no way.*

My Story through my Journaling and Self-talks.

Dedication

I want to dedicate this book to my mom and sisters who are all looking down on me from Heaven. I hope you guys are proud of the man I have become…

Contents

Intro- My Story through my journaling and self-talks 1

Chapter 1- As I walk with God 5

Chapter 2- He Loves Us in Spite of our Faults 7

Chapter 3- The Addiction 9

Chapter 4- The Suicidal Thoughts 12

Chapter 5- What's going on 14

Chapter 6- I am going to Fight a good Fight 18

Chapter 7- A Quick Journey 22

Chapter 8- A Family Affair 26

Chapter 9- The New Year 32

Chapter 10- Problems 36

Chapter 11- Open Your Eyes 39

Chapter 12- Choices 43

Chapter 13- Let Go and Let God 45

Chapter 14- Striving to Be a Better Christian 50

Chapter 15- Kingdom Men 54

Chapter 16- Birthday Travel 55

Chapter 17- Getting Ready for Heaven 58

Chapter 18- The Devil Is Busy 60

Chapter 19- My Mom Prayed for Me 64

Chapter 20- My Sobriety 67

Chapter 21- Catching Hell 72
Chapter 22- Blessed to be in the Number 77
Chapter 23- Giving Thanks 81
Chapter 24- Another New Year 85
Chapter 25- He showed up 88

INTRODUCTION

My Story through my Journaling and Self-talks.

Monday November 11, 2013

Good Monday morning, it is November 11, 2013 at 1:59 am; and I just got up to use the restroom and I laid back down and reflected back on yesterday morning. I woke up around 6am; I read the little pamphlet "Our Daily Bread". I also read a couple of pages of "Your Best Life Now" by Joel Osteen and I'm sitting on the side of the bed thinking about life and all I've went through.

I am thinking to myself, I have just been laid off from work for about two and a half weeks now. My bills are still rolling in; but I am trusting in God to bring me through.

Yesterday morning, I watched this gospel show called "Lift Every Voice", with Corey Condrey. They had a guest on the show by the name of Tameron Hall.

I think she is one of the most beautiful women in the world. I am asking God for a chance to meet her in person. She is smart, beautiful, and classy and is a dream come true for a man like me; Yes Lord, I would love to put a ring on her finger.

Wednesday November 13, 2013

Today is Wednesday, 13th and I got up around 6am. Every morning I try to thank God for letting me see another day. I also try to read the word every day and I learned, as long as I keep my focus on God, I'm good. There are some days that the Devil tries to get me sidetracked but, I just keep my mind focused on positive things."

My walk with God has been a battle but I know I am going to win this race because my God has all power.

* * *

Today was a good day, although I am still out of work and my bills are still coming in. I injured my finger and I am going to be in permanent pain for life.

My lawyer screwed me around and that is all right because I know God has my back because he lives in me and I am his child. I know that he will supply all my needs.

"God has told me a lot of things that I am supposed to be doing and I'm putting them in the making."

Michael's Tip #1- *When God tells you to do something, you better do it or deal with the outcome and that is usually not pretty.*

It is a shame when you call yourself a Christian and when things hit the fan your Christianity just disappear but, I'm not perfect either. I just try to keep it one hundred and real.

My niece and I are very close and we spent most of the day together. Although she gets on my nerves sometimes and I am sure I get her nerves sometimes too

Tuesday November 19th, 2013

Good morning it is Tuesday, November 19 4:21am. I got some issues going on with my stomach and my friends keep telling me I need to see a doctor.

I am scared but I made up my mind to make an appointment. Sometimes we just have to listen to people when they tell you something and especially when in our hearts we know that they are right.

Every Monday the church I attend has something called noonday prayer which usually lasts from 12 to 2pm supposedly but sometimes, the Lord says otherwise and it lasts longer. We always have a good time.

Reverend Patricia Miller speaks only what God has given her to say and what he has done in her life. If you did not know, we serve an awesome God; yes, we do.

Minister Stella Calvert and Sister Alice Jackson told me things that the Lord has said but, I am sometimes hard headed and stubborn to some of what was being said. Now I can admit that when things have happened, then and only then did I know my God was real.

So if you are reading this book

Michael's Tip #2: You had better know who God is. He is a healer, provider, doctor, lawyer, counselor, friend, father, and mother. He is everything only if you put your faith and trust in him.

Make sure that you know Him for yourself. Do you hear what I'm saying? He will never leave you nor forsake you.

The word: Psalms 150 says, "Praise ye the Lord. Praise God in his sanctuary: praise him in the firmament of his power. Praise him for his mighty acts: praise him according to his excellent greatness." "Praise him with the sound of the trumpet: praise him with the psaltery and harp. Praise him with the timbre and dance: praise him with stringed instruments and organs. Praise him upon the loud cymbals: praise him upon the high-sounding cymbals. Let everything that hath breath praise the LORD. Praise ye the LORD.

CHAPTER 1

As I walk with GOD

As I walk with God, I think back on how I could have made better decisions. If only I had listen to my mom and others telling me about the alcohol and drugs. I wanted to do what Michael wanted to do, although I know doing most of those things would have caused me headaches and pain, going to jail, and I knew I was hurting myself and others I cared about.

I still have trials and tribulations. However, it is all right because God said; lay all your troubles on me. I know he is real and got my back and if he did not I would have been in my grave long time ago or in prison somewhere.

So I want to say "Thank you God for your Grace and Mercy" and still allowing me to be here. Thank you Jesus, Glory is to God because he has everything you need and want.

Michael's Tip #3: First you have to accept God in your life and then walk the path that he wants you to walk.

In my first book, I spoke about how I started drinking and smoking at a very early age. If you are reading this book, please think before you pick up that first beer, cigarette, crack cocaine, acid, or any other harmful drug or alcohol. It is not worth it; trust me I have been down that road and done all of that and more.

I realized when the time was right that it was time for me to walk ***Michael's Tip* #4:** If you are out there and don't know what to do or where to go it's time to come in; let go and let God.

I know that God is the way, the truth, and the light.

I'm 48 years now, soon to be 49 on July 23rd and it took me until I was 41 years old to get it right. And the only reason it happened at that point is because I ended up in jail and was looking at prison for up to 30 years.

I then turned to my God for help and he answered my prayers. I promised Him, I will leave the drinking and drugs alone; and guess what I kept my word.

If God can take an alcoholic and drug addict like me and turn my life around; then He certainly can do the same for you. I'm a true man of God and I love every minute of it, but I do have lots of struggles still.

I know that I serve an awesome God, but one of my biggest problems is that I do not give God all the praises for what He has done for me. When I am in church, I am afraid to let go and give God the real praise the He deserves. I wonder what other people are going to think; I know that God is going to bring me out of that shyness. He knows that He got me. I will never leave Him again and I am going to keep on praising, worshipping and glorifying His holy and righteous name. I am so glad to be in the number.

CHAPTER 2

He loves us in Spite of our Faults

As we get older our bodies and our mind changes. It takes longer to heal; when we do not treat our bodies' right.

Michael's Tip #5: we need to remember to treat our bodies as the Lord's temple while we are young because you may not get a chance to fix it when you get older.

God loves use in spite of our faults. And I know that God put people in our lives to deter us from our own demise and you have to know when or when these people are God sent, because there are a lot of fake Christians just lurking to destroy our lives.

These people are not sent by God, but are sent by the devil. So make sure you are very careful seeking the real God. When you do, be truthful and faithful to his word and don't forget to be obedient.

Monday November 25th, 2013

Today is a great day, although I am still going through things.

I have to keep on trusting God because I know he is the ONLY ONE who is going to bring me through everything I'm going through right now.

There were times when I really felt like giving up and going back to my old ways but, I think about the close calls, bad and terrifying moments that God allowed me to get through and I just kept trusting and believing that He is going to do just what he says, He will do.

***Michael's Tip* #6:** Always Seek God's love and mercy!

Some things go along with walking with God. And I know It is not an easy walk but, it's worth every minute of your precious life. I mentioned that there were days that I felt like giving up, but God stuck with me and has brought me too far to turn back now.

I have a real good friend who is always telling me that life and death is in the tongue and as a matter of fact, I have heard a couple of people say the same thing. I have also read it in the bible. I have learned to be careful with the words that come out of my mouth. I realized that the tongue has a lot of evil in it and can cause a whole lot of hurt and pain, if you don't watch what comes out of your mouth. I have hurt a lot of people by saying stuff that I did know about and I did not care whether or not I was telling the truth. I just wanted to hurt that person at that moment and now I know because of my walk with God that is incorrect behavior. Through this God Loves me in spite of my faults.

CHAPTER 3

The addiction

As a young man, I wanted the best job, the biggest house, the nicest car, and the most beautiful wife on earth. Now do not get me wrong there is nothing wrong with wanting and having these things, but the magnitude that you have to go through to get them or keep them is where the line with God is drawn.

In addition, when you want to party, drink and everything that comes along with this package (you know what I am talking about) you will suffer the consequences that come along with that type of lifestyle.

What happened to me is I ended up letting my guard down and started running wild, drinking more heavily and using stronger drugs.

I ended up being addicted and ended up also being in denial about my addiction. And I did this for a long, long time.

If the first thing you grab in the morning, when you wake up, is alcohol; then you know you have a serious problem. I would not wish being an addict or alcoholic on any one because, once you are there, it is hard to come back to the basic life style. Take my word for it, I am a living witness. But Thanks be to God, He is my savior, healer, provider, friend, father, mother, sister, and brother in the time of need. Glory be to God. This is how I recovered.

And Now that God has spared my life to see the age of 48, I have learned so much. I now know that

Michael's Tip #7: You do not need nice thing, drugs or alcohol to please others or to fit in, but all you need is Jesus to be the head of your life.

I am a living testament. I was at rock bottom. He picked me up and turned me around. I am now a born again Christian. Although I am not perfect, I can be the person that God wants me to be. Every now and then, I catch myself thinking about grabbing a cold beer; I cannot go back to that kind of life style so I stop because the addiction is always lurking somewhere. I am so glad that the old Michael is gone and that God changed my life to be a better person and better man. I know I am going to make it because I am putting all my trust in God. With God's help, I am going to fight whatever the Devil tries to bring my way. I know what I did in the past does not matter to God because He got me and I am going to let my light shine where I go.

There were times when I thought I would lose my mind and there were times when I thought that I would not amount to anything. I really wanted to change, but I didn't know how to do it. The crack cocaine had really took over my life. I use to beg God to deliver me from my addiction. I use to cry myself to sleep at nights. My addiction was destroying my life.

When I was in my own little world, I wanted to have the nice home, beautiful wife and family; but every time I got money in my pocket, it was as if I got that butterfly feeling in my gut. I was getting the urge and the money was burning a hole in my pocket and because I was an addict the drug would be calling me in other words.

Then I would call someone for a ride because I did not have a vehicle or driver's license because of my addiction. While being an addict I was just existing. Also as an addict, I would say to myself that I just need one twenty dollar crack rock and deep down I knew that was not going to work once I took that first hit.

I would spend all the money I had in my pocket; then I would try to get some on credit. I use to run around looking crazy because being a crack addict causes paranoia and has your eyes all wide opened because you are thinking that everybody is looking at and watching you.

That crack will destroy you and take everything you have and own and I mean everything, house, car, family, money and most of all your life.

CHAPTER 4

The suicidal thoughts

I can remember when I use to think about committing suicide ALL THE TIME.

I was so confused and tired because I was drinking and using drugs all the time and I just wanted to "GIVE UP".

I had low self-esteem because I did not know what to do and I did not care about myself. And on top of that, which now I know was the "devil" kept telling myself that I was less than everybody else and I wasn't worth anything. However, thanks to God, I had a caring and praying mother that loved me despite all my bad decisions. Even though at times I did not return the love to her, she never gave up on me. Thinking back now, I was just plain out stupid for many of the things I did.

***Michael's Tip* #8:** When you do not have the right relationship with God, it is hard to have the right relationship with anyone else.

I use to talk back to my mom all the time knowing I was not raised that way but I did what I wanted to do. However, because God was still in my soul despite where I was, I knew deep down inside I was wrong.

I had these constant thoughts of suicide because I let the alcohol and drugs abuse get the best of me and I was in a dark place for a very long time, but God spared me.

***Michael's Tip* #9:** Those suicidal thoughts are the devil and if you have those thoughts, you need to seek God immediately. He held the key to my life and holds the key to yours.

CHAPTER 5

What's going on

My teenage years were much different from the teens of today. They are much more advanced and the world has a lot to offer them. I also look around and see that there is so much violence, crimes with young and old, schools, movie theaters, malls, clubs, and the killing of kids and seniors.

It is just a shame and that is why you need to always walk with God and watch whom you are around because it only takes a minute to be in the wrong place at the wrong time and that will change your life forever.

***Michael's Tip* #10:** Some friends are not really your friend and sometimes you have to cut them loose as well as some family members too if they do not mean you any good.

Thursday November 28, 2013

Today is November 28, 2013, Thanksgiving Day. I often wonder are we really thankful for the things we have. Sometimes I lose focus on what God has blessed me with just like everyone else. I know I should be thankful just because he gave me life for 48 years and a mom who loved me. God bless her soul, she died in 1993. I am also thankful for my daddy who died in 1972. Most of all I am thankful to God for being free of alcohol and drugs, not incarcerated or in my grave. I am thankful God gave me food to eat, a roof over my head, and everything else I have.

There are days when I sit and think about what I have and what I want and then I catch myself. I know that there are people who have nowhere to go or food to eat. And I think to myself, here I am complaining about not having stuff I don't need, but I know I just need to be thankful for what I have and be happy in my current state.

One of the main things that I want to do in my life now is to get closer and build my trust and faith with God and be obedient in his word. I want to serve God with all my heart, mind, soul, and strength.

I have been going through some health issues for quite some time now and have been trying to figure out what is going on. I thought it was my kidney or bladder because I could not empty my bladder at one point and once I went to the doctor then I found out that my prostate was enlarged.

When I would go to the doctor, he would give me some medicine and I would take it until it runs out but I would never go back for a follow up and then I realized I was not getting well.

Now it seems like I am going through something again. When I go to the bathroom I feel like I cannot urinate and it sometimes takes 20 to 30 minutes.

Saturday November 30, 2013

Today I have had enough and I went to the emergency room. I got there around 2pm and when I spoke to the nurse and doctor, I explained to them what was going on with me.

I was given a cup to provide a urine sample, but I tried and tried and nothing came out and I knew deep down this was not good.

***Michael's Tip* #11:** If you are going through some medical issues, I suggest you go and get checked out immediately. Health waits for no man.

I was wondering what was going on and I kept on thinking about my beautiful daughter and my four grandchildren and how badly I want to see them grow up.

I kept thinking God is going to turn this around. I told the doctor that I could not urinate and she insisted that I not leave without doing a urine check to find out if my kidney was infected.

She then said she would put a catheter in, in which I had never done or even heard about for that matter.

The nurse finally came back to explain the process and they started the catheter. It was so painful and unlike any pain that I had experienced. But in the mist of it all I kept praying and all I could say to myself is Lord please help me and I knew I was going to be alright.

I felt uncomfortable for the first 5 minutes, but once the nurse got the catheter in, the urine started to flow in the bag. I definitely would not want to go through that process again. And once the urine collection was finally over and test were completed; the doctor came in to speak with me and ended up prescribing me something called Flow-max, which is a drug for an enlarged prostate.

….Let me tell you how good God is. I took the prescription to Walmart to be filled and when I asked how much it was going to cost the lady at the counter told me $65.00. Then I was thinking to myself I do not have any money because I had been laid off from my job for a little over a month now.

….Then I proceeded to ask her if I could please purchase five or six of the pills just to get started. She then said yes and told me it would be $10.00 and $10.60 total with tax.

So I started thinking I have no money. Although it is only $10 I still do not have it, but then I went to my niece to borrow the money and she gave it to me.

When I got home, I ate and took one of my prescribed pills. The directions said to take one every 30 minutes after I ate.

But guess what happened???? When I opened the prescription bottle, I found out that the woman at the pharmacy filled the entire prescription.

Glory be to God. It was not anybody but God and I learned at that moment I just have to ***Michael's Tip* #12** Remember to walk in faith and stop worrying, let God handle your problems.

I know he is going to bring me through all of this. I was referred to an urologist for a follow up in which I will definitely go.

CHAPTER 6

I am going to fight a good fight

Tuesday December 3, 2013

Good morning, it is early Tuesday morning, December 3, 2013 at 1:05am. I have now learned how to listen to other Christians give their testimony.

I now know that everything we go through is only a test of our faith and for us to stay connected to God and his holy word.

There are times when I know I want to give up and ask God why me and why do I have to go through this, but now I know it is only a test to see how I am going to respond and act.

"God I am going to fight a good fight until the end. I know I got a blessing coming and most of all you get the honor, glory and praise; thank you Jesus."

As I go through life, I know things will not always go the way I want them to, but I will continue to keep on holding to God's unchanging hands.

I have a greater purpose in life and I want to serve God with respect, honesty and dignity.

He made me and without Him I'm nothing. God put others in your life for a reason and one of the people he put in my life is an awesome friend.

Sometimes when she calls my phone, I do not feel like picking up and she usually leaves a message saying, "oh you are too busy to answer or you are probably talking to another woman."

And usually my phone would be in another room or on silent. She is a real talker and there are some days I just do not want to talk to her, but I know this is not of God.

This sometimes happens for weeks and my heart usually tells me that I need to apologize to her, so I do and this usually always makes me feel better.

There are often times when God will tell me to do things and I do not do it; but I know I need to be obedient to my master's word.

I think to myself, how can you not serve a God like this? Once you try Him you will NEVER go back unless you don't want to have great things happen in your life.

A little gospel: I came to tell you to get real and get on the battlefield for your God. I am getting to the point that I am going to let little light of mine shine and let him fight all my battles.

Why, because He is a God who cannot lose no matter how great the fight is and I can not do this on my own.

I know you heard this saying "No weapon formed against me shall prosper" and "I'm more than a conqueror".

Have you ever wondered why you hold on to the past?

I have been doing it all my life and I did not know why. It was not doing me any good. It was just holding me back from where I wanted to go and this could be a big hindrance in your life if you are holding on to the past.

In my drinking and drug days, I did not think about my problems. Everything I was going through was only getting worst because all I wanted to do was drink and get high. I was a young father, 18 years old and I did not even want to work. I was going nowhere but that is all I wanted to do. I did not want to take responsibility for my actions and when I got into trouble, I would always run home to mom, even though most of the time I was disrespectful.

She took me in when my birth mom put me up for adoption and especially because she is no longer here TODAY, I still regret not respecting her.

Listen to me young and old, male or female:

***Michael's Tip* #13:** Honor your mother and father, no matter what you are going through.

When they tell you something and you do not agree with them, keep your mouth closed and move on.

In my situation, my mom always told me things that were a benefit to me, but I wanted to do what Michael wanted to do and always got in trouble or held back because I was rude and disrespectful. Remember: God will not bless this type of behavior.

I'm telling you to be thankful for everything and know that God allows you to go through things for a reason and this is to make you better and stronger. Do not take my word for it; take God's word, because He does not lie. I have tried Him and still trying Him. And no matter what I go through, now I can handle it without drugs and alcohol. If I want to be blessed, I have to roll with God Almighty and you should too.

* * *

I am leaving to go to Pittsburg, Pennsylvania on Sunday morning. My two nephews and brother-in-law will be going also. I have been watching the weather and it's very cold and snowing up there. I am just praying that we make it there safe. It's been quite a while since I've been up North; looking forward to this trip."

CHAPTER 7

A Quick Journey

Sunday December 8th, 2013

We left about 10am Sunday morning. It rained all the way to Washington, DC. We ran into traffic, the roads were icy and covered in snow on both sides of the road. It was a messy trip but we arrived safely around 11:30pm.

We stayed at my brother's dad house. It sounds funny but we have the same mother, but different fathers. My mom put me up for adoption but he always treated me as if I was his own.

On Monday morning, after we were up, he had breakfast already made for us. We got dressed and went site seeing. It was a good day. We took many pictures like the Pittsburg Steelers Stadium mountains views and other stuff like that.

We ended up going to Pennsylvania for our job, which was to correct some work in Hershey. However, what we needed to get to do the job was not going to be ready until that Wednesday. Therefore, we ended up staying in Pittsburg until that Wednesday and we left Hershey that afternoon. The few days we stayed in Pittsburg we went to the casino and we had a blast.

That Wednesday evening we arrived in Hershey around 6pm or so. We checked into the hotel and grabbed something to eat and then we relaxed for the rest of the night. On Thursday, we got up early and prepared for work. After breakfast, we drove to the plant where we met the boss. About half way through the job, all work was stopped on the project because, we encountered another problem.

We ended up having to drive back to Charleston for a few days. We left Pennsylvania around 12pm that afternoon and arrived in Charleston around 10pm that Thursday night. This was another long drive and we will drive back to Pittsburgh on next Wednesday.

I am still dealing with some health issues but I know that God is going to bring me through it. I just have to keep holding on because I want to see my grandchildren grow up and be successful.

There are still many things I want to do like, getting married and owning my own home. I need privacy because I have been staying with someone else.

My dream:

I would like to come home from church; my wife and I will enjoy a nice dinner together, we would have nice conversations about our awesome God, and just cuddle. We would talk about all the great things that He has done and going to do in our lives. I want my own home, beautiful, true women of God, to have my grandchildren back in my life and a better relationship with my beautiful daughter.

Right now I am hoping and believing God is going to bring everything that He has promised to me. In my mind: I will receive it very soon.

Many nights I get lonely, I feel like I just want to go out or call a friend up and take it to another level, but I am trying to hold on to God's word, but it does get very hard.

So I am trusting that God will answer all of my prayers if I just keep the faith and believe in His word.

I have been struggling pretty much, all my life but brought most of it on myself by wanting to do things my way. I can take ownership because I messed my own bed up but thanks to GOD now I am getting my life back right. I am living for God now but there are many things that I have to correct and get right still.

Sunday December 15th, 2013

Today is Sunday, December 15th and the pastor was talking about how our life can be a mess. I am still in this mode that looks like when I get out of one mess I go right to another.

I remember back in the day when I use to think about suicide and wanted to end my life because I thought less of myself. I did not have as much as the other young kids that I grew up with but, now I am glad I did not go through with it because it was only the wicked Devil trying to make me ruin my life and throw my life away. I did not have as much as the other kids but I had a mother who loved me and now that I am older and have God as the head of my life. Love is a whole lot better to have then material things. Love conquers all and love is what makes the world go around.

My life has been a real struggle from my alcohol and drug use. I was addicted to these deadly substances for years. I let my past ruin my life by constantly dwelling on the past. I just fed on it worrying and thinking about my past instead of moving on with my future. Now I live for God and I know if I do not I would be back in the world partying, drinking, drugging and probably dead if you want to know the truth.

* * *

My mom was born in 1904 and passed in 1993. It's been twenty years and I still miss her and think about her like it was yesterday. My mom was a loving and wonderful woman that I will never forget. Why do we want to grow up before our time and do things that we are not supposed to do? Well, I can't answer for no one but me. I did it because I wanted attention, to fit in with my friends, to be talked about and stand out from the rest: I wanted to fit in, but as we, all know that does not last long. A Quick Journey is not always good.

CHAPTER 8

A Family Affair

Monday December 16th, 2013

It is Monday, December 16 and 1:05 in the morning. I had gotten up to use the bathroom and I had laid back down. I was thinking that when you get a certain age, you should make a change in your life and a change to be a better person.

You should change from doing people wrong, from drinking and smoking and making a positive change in your life as well as to help other people in their lives.

We should influence other people who do not think life is worth living because we are all God's children and no matter what we have or what we have done no one has the right to judge other people.

I often ask myself who are we to judge one another? I have family members who are always talking about my mom; who she was and who she was not. Like they have never done wrong to anyone. And I have always been known to be a quiet person, but if I wasn't trying to live like God wanted me to live and love everyone; I would have already drugged him.

* * *

It's been twenty years since my mom passed and I have family members that are still talking about her. So to me family is not always the best and I know this statement will step on someone toes, but oh well, when dealing with family even if it hurts their feelings stuff has to be said.

Additionally, I have some family members who will say that they are proud of me for turning my life around and how much they love me and then I have another set of family members who only looks down on me and that's fine too because I cannot continue to live my life thinking about what others think about me.

* * *

See I moved from Georgia back in 2013 and I have very few family members who have called and see how I was doing. And we all know family is not at all they pretend to be! Everything that glitters is not gold, trust me on that one. I had people who aren't related to me treat me better than my own family, but it really doesn't matter to me anymore because I got a friend, a savior, a healer, a provider that does everything for me; He's my everything, and He is my way maker. The only thing that man can do for us is lie. Let them say what they want, it is what it is. After 48 years I have finally put God back in my life and that is the best thing I have ever done?

If our family member or friends have a problem with that, tell them to take it up with God almighty and let them see who will have the last word.

***Michael's Tip* #14**: No one is mightier than God and I encourage you to stay focus on the Lord and He can bring you through any rain or thunderstorm.

He has brought me through many, many terrible storms and he is going to bring me through many, many more as long as I keep holding on to his unchanging hands. It is now 1:40 am on Monday morning and it is time for me to go back to bed to see if I can get some rest. Goodnight now and have a bless night.

* * *

Good morning, it is Tuesday morning and I have a doctor's appointment today. I am a little afraid because of the problems I am having. I do not want to hear that I have a serious problem, but I know if I want to live long and be healthy I got to start living right and taking care of myself. I am a young black African American and I have to keep checking on my health by getting checked by a doctor. So men if you don't want to have a problem, don't wait too late to get checked by a doctor

***Michael's Tip* #15:** Please make it a point to have your annual check-up every year and take care of yourself so you can live a healthy spiritual life.

* * *

Today is Christmas Eve and I have been out of work for a while. I feel bad because it is one day before Christmas and I don't have any gifts for my grandchildren because I don't have any money right now. I am just praying and asking God for a financial break through.

I have always tried to get all four of them something and I know that they will be looking for something from their granddad. Deep down inside I am hurting because I cannot get them anything but, I do have one gift that money cannot buy and that is that I am praying for them and my daughter that God send his angels down to keep them safe from harm's way.

It is 7:03am December 24 and I am up watching Joseph Prince Ministry. The topic was God is for you today. It was music to my ears and mind because I need Him every day because I cannot make it without Him.

I said something earlier that sometimes you have to cut some of your family members off to be in a better position for yourself. And I'm going to say this again…It is sad that sometimes strangers will help you before your family member does, but we can't choose our families and the way I'm wired I am still going to keep on pressing until the end with or without them.

I also know that when it comes to family I have let my kindness turn into weakness and sometimes I do too much for some. I know that God has my best interest at heart. I am not perfect and I make plenty of mistakes but I am trusting and believing that God will bring me through everything that I am going through. I just have to stay focused on Him and have faith in His work and sometimes we just have to leave family where they are.

* * *

I have another sister who have been going through chemotherapy and she has been handling this pretty good. She was doing well. I text and called her pretty often recently, but I was not getting an answer to my text or calls. I was worried. Then my brother, Jerry called me to tell me that our sister was sent over into hospice care and the doctor gave her 3 months to live. I was hurt and shocked. I cried mostly all night, but I managed to go to work the next day. I was trying to talk to God because I could not understand it; I was mad and asking God why? After I calmed down, then it came to me, why was I questioning God. God is God. I did not have the right to question Him. He is my maker as well as my sister's. He is the creator. He rules the heavens and the earth. Now I was mad at myself. I have to watch what comes out of my mouth. He knows what is best for her and if He wanted to take my sister home with Him; then I will still praise Him. I will still give Him glory and if He let her live a little longer then I would love that too.

* * *

I use to be a deadbeat dad and I know that my alcoholic and drug problems kept me out of my daughter's life, but thanks to God, we have started the healing process together. We are back talking and my grandkids are back in my life. I love them all very, very much. When my daughter and I have disagreements, she would often bring up my past. It hurts because I have apologized over and over again for my past however I'm never going to be tired of apologizing, because I brought this on myself and I don't even blame her. I know now I have to put it in God's hands and I know it will get fixed because God fixed me. I needed major work done on me. He is the only one who can do it. I am just waiting and trusting in my God for a whole lot things like my finances, homes, health and my wife. I really hate that I missed most of my daughter's childhood years because of my addiction, but I know it is done now and I have to go on with the rest of my life to better myself. I couldn't kick my bad habits by myself and if it wasn't for the Lord on my side to keep me strong and for putting real Christian people in my life to correct me.

* * *

I want to thank my mom, Mrs. Pearlie Burton for all that she had done and poured in me. She made a big difference in my life. She kept telling me how good God is; I am happy that she took my brother and me to church every Sunday night. We made stops to see people here or there and now that I am older, I have learned to appreciate everything she did and told me.

Family is not always, what we want but they are all we have so we have to learn to deal with it and Thank God for them anyway.

CHAPTER 9

The New Year

Today is January 1, 2014 and God has blessed me to see another year. I thought I was not going to make it through 2013 but God had other plans for me. I have made some New Year's resolution and I am going to stick to them because I am trying to better my life and get the things that God has for me. I am going to be obedient to His words and follow his commandments.

In 2013, I did many things that I should not have done. This year is my season to really trust God and really be blessed. I want to meet my wife, get my own place and serve God with all my heart. I just want to give Him all of me and serve Him like I never did before.

Last night at church was amazing. There was a lot of people giving their testimonies on how good, awesome and what God has done for them. And when I heard their testimony, it just made me want to serve him more. It made me forget about my problems and everything else I was going through. I wanted God to take me places that I have never experienced.

* * *

Today is the first Sunday of the year and I am glad I made it through another year and I am going to put my trust in God and stop trying to work things out as I tried to do last year. I knew what I was doing because I needed God to work some things out in my life; I do not want 2014 to be like 2013. Therefore, I am asking God, to be debt free, in good health and to be closer to my daughter and granddaughter. I have also asked God to give me strength and knowledge to be right with Him and do His will.

* * *

Today's sermon was on "Change" and change is very good. I went through many changes, many years not thinking about changing for the better. I just wanted to do what Michael wanted to do and it kept leading me down the wrong path. The path of drinking, drugging, hanging out, and being disrespectful to my mom.

Thank God that I am now clean and sober. I have made many changes. The alcohol and crack for starters as of this date, **January 2014, is now seven years, four months and five days behind me.** I use to stay in trouble, watching pornography, lying all the time and just doing things God was not pleased with.

* * *

Today the choir was very good. I never thought that I would be serving God like I do; I just want to give Him all of me and I want all of Him because I know through God, He can take me to higher heights and even places I can't imagine.

In 2014 this New Year, I am going to press my way through to stay focused on my Jesus and serve Him until the day I die, but I know that

I will have trials and tribulations but God has all powers and I will make it through.

There were many times that I brought things and struggles on myself and I was angry and blamed God for my mistakes. Often times we will call on God in times of troubles but in reality, we need to call on Him every day because He holds the key to everything rather it is Good or Bad. He is our savior and healer. He is our everything.

***Michael's Tip* #16:** Now is the time to give God your life and watch what He will do for You.

* * *

Good morning its early Monday 1:50 am, January 6 and once again I had gotten up to use the bathroom and went back to bed. I could not go back to sleep. I kept hearing the Lord saying, "Get up and write". So here I am telling and hoping I am influencing someone to change their life style, to change the way they talk, the way they act, to put God ahead of their lives because it is so much better to serve the Lord than the Devil. I did not say that it is going to be easy, but with God in the mist, you will come first every time.

I try to read out of my Daily Bread every morning and one Sunday morning as I was reading, at the end of the page it said, "When life feels like a storm-tossed sea, with crashing waves of pain and grief, turn to the Lord and trust Him. He will give you peace and bring relief. It is better to go through the storm with Jesus Christ than to have smooth sailing without Him" and that is the truth. I am telling you this and if you do not know, God is real.

I cause a lot of trouble and hell for myself because I did not listen to my mom and others who tried to tell me right from wrong. Thanks be to God that I am still breathing and walking around.

* * *

I have been shot at and the bullet went right by my head. I have had a gun put right in front of my head. I have been in car wrecks where my head went through the windshield. I've been told to lay face down on the ground, me and a few friends but, I took off running and the guys caught me in the church yard and roughed me up. God gets all the glory because you know how that was supposed to end. I know it was not anybody but God, nothing but His grace and mercy.

The time when I was drinking and smoking crack heavily, I would hear bells ringing and then everything would go black. I was too stupid to realize I was about to end my life because I choose to still drink and get high. I know that God has me here for a reason.

***Michael's Tip* #17:** Give your life to Christ; you cannot go wrong doing this, besides He rules everybody and everything. So give Him a chance.

I did and look at me now, although I still have my days, I know God is my breadwinner and He is going to see me through so I am going to continue to trust and believe Him.

CHAPTER 10

Problems

Today is Saturday, January 11, 6:48am. When I think about my life and where I use to be; who I am now, I can truly say that I am blessed. I use to be tore up from the floor up and now I am a changed man for the better.

On my last job, I cut my right index finger, almost all the way off and I had to get it reattached and treated. It is permanently impaired and now my lawyer is going after the company. I remember my supervisor telling my coworkers that I meant to do it just to get a check, but I was thinking to myself who would do that for a check and then it came to me that yeah some people would do just that or more for a check. And once again I had to put it in God's hand because God knows better and that is all that matters. I believe that the company wanted to let me go anyway.

Do you know that people in this world will say anything to hurt someone else even if it is not true? My lawyer told me that my finger is damaged for life and he would get me a favorable settlement. Well, I signed the paperwork so that he could get his fee, then later on everything changed. I only got a settlement for what I would have gotten without a lawyer.

Lesson learned people are crooks.

And until this date I do not know what happened and I don't know if he sold me out or what, but I do know that God continues to bless me with what I was supposed to have and that is why I put my trust ONLY in Him. God is my doctor, my lawyer, my father, my healer and my savior; God is my everything.

* * *

It is now Saturday night 8:23pm and today was a slow day. I went to work from 7pm to 11am and after that, I went back to my brother's house to take a shower.

I went to the barbershop to get a trim for church tomorrow; then went to pay my phone bill and then back to my brother's house. There is nothing like your own because there is only so much you can do when you are living with someone, but I know this is a temporary situation and I thank him for allowing me to stay with him. Today I feel like giving up but God has brought me too far for me to turn back. So I am trusting in Jesus because I know that He is a healer, provider and savior; Thank God for His grace and mercy.

There are times when I would complain a lot, then I realized that someone did not wake up this morning, I did. The point is that God woke me up this morning with no worries, debt free and well taken care of. I can bless someone else who may need something to brighten up his or her day or simply just help. To let them know that someone else cares about them and that God is in the mist of it all.

It is a fact that if you do not have God's love then you have no love at all. If I do not have God, then I have nothing and will never reach my full potential without Him. I am giving God all the honor, praise and glory because if it had not been for His grace and mercy I would have been in jail or somewhere in my grave. My God still allows me to breathe. I serve an awesome God and if you do not know, you had better ask somebody. My day has come to an end, until I start up writing again you be a true believer of God and stay grounded and prayed up in His word. You be blessed in Jesus Name…Amen.

CHAPTER 11

Open your eyes

Today is Saturday, January 18, 4:58pm. I lost one of my sisters last year in July to lung cancer. She was 82. The doctor had gave her very little time to live, but she out lived what the doctor said.

I know God had the last say so that is why we must put our trust totally in God.

I had another sister who called me last year and told me that the doctor diagnosed her with stomach cancer. She went through chemotherapy treatment for so many weeks and just the other day, she texted me to say that one of the cancer cells had disappeared and the other one is shrinking. You know that God is so good all the time. We should just be thankful for being alive and able to breathe.

There are so many other things I want to be doing with life. I like going to work, church and home, I want to do more. I want to be a blessing to others, I love helping people in need. I want to better myself to be closer and stronger in the word of God. I want to achieve my goals to go further than I think I can go.

I know God has already fixed my situation no matter how big the problem may look.

Let me ask you a question, why do we do things when we know it is the wrong thing do?

The reason why I did was because I wanted people to recognize me and talk about me. Now that I am walking with Christ, I see things more differently now. I know life is so much better when we walk with God. I also know that trouble is so easy to get into but so hard to get out of. I have brought so much pain and heartache on myself that it did not even make sense anymore. I have learned from my mistakes. I am so thankful that there is a God and if it were not for Him, I would be dead or in prison somewhere.

* * *

Today is Sunday, January 19, we had a great speaker at our church today, and she was off the chain. The topic today was "Open Your Eyes". The spirit was very high. She said open your eyes to God and see what He has for you and where He wants to take you. I loved that topic because I want God to take me places that I have never been before. I want to be a blessing to other people. I want to teach them to put their trust and belief in the almighty God and tell them without Him we are nothing and without Him we will never be anything. I need to keep my focus on Jesus, study and feed on His holy word on the daily basis. I know I stray away from reading and studying the bible, from time to time, but I know I just have to stay with it, if I am going to be all I can be in Jesus' name. He is my rock and my strength in time of need.

Right now, I have a few family members that I am around that do a lot of cussing that I would rather not be around. I don't want you to say "oh he think he's all that", no I'm not, I'm not perfect and never will be, I've been there and done that and it got me nowhere. I love them dearly and wish the best for them. I cannot make them do anything they do not want to do. I can tell them do not be like I used to be and that is disrespectful, a trouble maker, an alcoholic and a drug addict. I want to encourage them to follow their dreams and make them come true. In order to do that, you have to have God in the mist of it all because without Him you are fighting a losing battle. I personally know this for myself. I know now that everything God has for me, I want it all and more abundantly.

A friend of mines, Sister Alice Jackson and Danus, we were all on a three-way phone call today; the conversation came up and I was told it is better to have a true friend for only a season than to have a fake friend for life. I agreed with that because when a true friend tells you something and it is for your good then soak it up and keep it moving. Oh yes sir because I got to win this race and let God know that He's my hero, my savior, my healer, and my everything. I thank God for the blessed Sunday that He has let me see. I am getting ready to lay down for tonight. I trust that you will stay prayed up, stay in the word and keep on feeding on God for whatever you are going through.

* * *

Today is January 28, 2014 and today in Charleston the weather is pretty bad. Some of the roads are closed. My job is also closed for today. It is going to be rough tomorrow because I will need to work that much longer to catch up. I also started a second job and I need to be working from 3pm-11pm. I am not trying to mess this job up because a good friend got me the job. If I was that old person I use to be, I would have said "just forget it, he'll be alright". I am just so grateful for the people who have helped me because we all need somebody in these days and times.

Have you ever wondered if you should really ask God, "do I really want to do your will and be able to get everything you have for us or do we pretend to serve Him until we get what we want from Him"?

I do not know about you, but I love serving God because He is the best thing that ever happened to me. I would not give that up for anything because He's everything that I need to be and then some. When things get hard and I cannot go on I just got to believe and trust in God, He will make away.

I am still having problems with my stomach, I am believing and trusting in Jesus to heal me of whatever is going on. He said that we are healed by His stripes and those are His words and I believe Him. I serve a God who does not lie and I know that He is a healer and a deliverer. He can make a way out of no way, especially if we open our eyes.

CHAPTER 12

Choices

It is Thursday, February 13, 9:46pm and I have slacked up on my writing. I've been blessed with another job that I work during the day until about 2pm and I need to be at the second job at 3pm until 11pm or later, especially on Tuesday's and Saturday's when we sometimes get off at 2 or 3 in the morning. I am usually tired and do not feel much like writing. I also have to get back reading my word too. I am also having problems with my hands. The doctor said I have carpal tunnel.

* * *

Today is Sunday, February 16 and my day started good. I got up around 7:30am. I started getting ready like every other morning, grabbed some breakfast and cleaned up my car before I went to church.

After ironing my clothes, I headed to church, got there around 11:05am. Sunday school was still going on, so I sat on the wall until church started. The subject of today's sermon is "Choices". Pastor Holt did a really nice job, church was off the chain.

As I reflected back over my lifestyle and thought about the choices that I have made. I only wish that I had found God sooner. God brought me through all of my bad choices and I know it was not nobody but Him.

If it was not for His grace and mercy I would be dead because of my choices, but Thank God I am free. I give Him all the praise and glory.

I have been asking God for a vehicle because I really need transportation to get around. In addition, there is nothing like having your own car to get back and forth to church and work, but once again, my choices have me in this predicament.

I was looking around for a car, my credit is so bad, and no one was willing to take a chance on me. But, thanks to God one day my nephew called to say that he had talked to someone at CarMax and he said that he could get me approved.

He got me on a three-way phone call and I spoke with the sales clerk. He asked me some questions and he said that he would give me a call back. Within ten minutes, I got a call from the salesperson that said if I put a down payment of $1,000 he could get me approved. I went to take him the money, I signed some papers and I left smiling and driving my own car. With the credit I have, it was nobody but Jesus.

***Michael's Tip* #18:** Even with bad choices with God on your side, anything is possible.

CHAPTER 13

Let go and Let God

I have been praying for a long time for God to allow me to be debt free. I want God to strengthen me all over, to create in me a clean heart and to renew my mind. I have to surrender my all and all to my Lord because I want to be a powerful man of God and to be obedient to His word and do his will.

I am ready and willing to let go and let God work things out and for me to have life more abundantly. I am also asking His healing power. *I know that greater is He who is in me than He that is in the world. I also know that no weapon formed against me shall prosper. I am a conqueror and I can do all things through Christ that strengthens me.*

* * *

Today is Monday, February 17th and my day started off pretty early. I usually get up around 6am; today I got up at 5am. I went to pick up my nephew and we got to work around 7:15am. My day ended around 2:20pm. I got to my other job around 3pm. I was a little tired and very hungry. I have not eaten since breakfast. I need to start eating properly and do my exercise; haven't started either one yet.

There is so many things going on and people are dying young and old. I am trying to live a long and healthy life. I guess I better stop talking about it and do something about it huh?

* * *

Today is March 7, 2014 and I thank God for blessing me to see another day. This week has been up and down. I mean when things are going good and in your favor, the Devil is always trying to throw things in your pathway to keep you distracted. Watch out for that!!!

I recently purchased a new vehicle. The car was running good and I was enjoying getting to work every day without any car worries. Tuesday night I went outside and low and behold somebody had hit my car and ran. I know that I am not perfect and I will never be, but that was very low down; I would never have done anything like that. I am very thankful that God changed me and my life for the better. I am going to continue to put God first and be obedient to His word.

Friday morning a friend of mine called to say a lady we both knew died from a heart attack. She lived in Georgia. I was not sure how true that was. Therefore, I called my niece, but she had not heard anything.

She made some calls and I found out it was true. This young woman was like a sister to me because my mom helped raised her. She was not much older than I was. In addition to having that on my mind, another young woman I knew died earlier this morning from lung cancer. She had been going through chemotherapy and this woman was just like a mother to me.

We often called and checked on one another. I called her last week and spoke with her son who said that she was under the weather. Her meds was recently changed by her doctor; and that day she was not feeling well. I had promised to go see her last Sunday after church, and I did not make it. This taught me a lesson not to put things off. If you keep putting things off for another time, something like this could happen and this could leave you feeling very bad; life is short.

God gave us two dates; the day of our birth and the day we die. We need to stay prayed up and continue to thank God for life while the blood is still running warm in our veins. We do not know the hour, day or time when God will close our eyes for the last time. Either you will be in heaven or hell, the choice is yours.

I know I am not where I want to be, but I am going to trust God to His word on everything He promised.

The word: Matthew 6:33 says, "Seek ye first the kingdom of God and His righteousness will be unto you".

I am trusting God; it is the only way for me. I know without God I am nothing and without Him, I will never be anything.

* * *

Today is Tuesday, March 11, 2014, as I sit here thinking about all the things that God has brought me through. As I look back over my past and life, I would have done things a lot different. I cannot change that now, I can however change the way I live the rest of my life and the only way to change for the better is to put the all mighty God first in my life.

I tried Him and I got hooked on Him real bad. That is a good thing. When I was drinking and getting high, I thought that high was good, but the high of Jesus is out of this world. He can heal your sickness, you being bored and your debts. He can do anything that your heart desires.

***Michael's Tip* #19:** God is the best remedy ever; I encouraged you to get hooked on Jesus because He is all the alcohol and drugs you'll ever need.

* * *

Today is Sunday, April 6 and I have not been writing like I should. I know when you have in your mind to do something the Devil comes at you to inconvenience you. He keep giving me excuses, wait on tomorrow or you know that you are not feeling good today. By then 2-4 days have went by and I have not gotten back to reading. I have told myself and try to motivate myself to do things because if I do not I will never do it. I have so many things that I want to do for God and so many things that I want and need Him to bless me with. There are some things that I have been doing and in God's eyes I know that it is not in His will. I have stopped doing those things because I put God first. I know I need to pray and trust in my master's plan; the plan He has for my life. I know prayer works. If it did not, I would not be here today.

Thank God for showing me favor. I am trusting and holding on to God's unchanging hands. I know that I can do all things through Jesus Christ who strengthens me.

As I go through life wondering what and if I will ever succeed in the things that I want in life. I have to remember that God already has a plan for my life and the only thing I need to do is to let go and let God have His way. Sometimes we get in God's way and mess things up, I am getting better and learning how to lean more on God and not onto my own understanding.

CHAPTER 14

Striving to be a better Christian

It is Sunday, April 13th and the last two days was great. I am going through something but thanks be to God for His grace and mercy, for waking me up this morning.

I am so thankful for that. I still have a few health problems, but I know my God can heal me because He said so in His word that I am healed by His stripes. He is a God that cannot lie. I will continue to trust and hold on to His word for doing greater and more powerful things in my life.

He my God with all power, not a little power; but, total power. I know that I have to stand still and know that He is God almighty.

I know that sometimes we let things get in our minds and we get sidetracked. Well I know that is how I get sometimes. I believe I have a true heart of gold but, sometimes my mind let bitterness and anger at people get me trapped and I know this is not the way.

I know that I need to stay focused on the word of God if I want to win this table. I need to continue to hang around Godly people and stay in God's word on a daily basis. I know that once you get in that dark tunnel it is hard to get out. Trust me I know. When I was down that lonely dark road, it was very scary. Thanks be to God for His favor for bringing me out. I did not want to die on that road and go to Hell. I encourage you to turn your life around and over to God if you intend to see God Almighty because what a mighty God we serve.

* * *

Today is a good day. I am putting my trust and faith in God. It is not where it should be yet, I am going to keep on trusting in His word because He is a God that can't lie and I am a man that is going to trust God for all that I need and want.

God said, "To seek first the Kingdom of Heaven and all the other things shall be added unto you". I know He is going to do what He said He would do. My God is a miracle worker and I know He can do the impossible. However, we have to be patient, because when it does not happen when we think it should happen, the Devil will try to convince us that God has forgotten about us, but deep down inside we know that God is still on the throne sitting high and looking low.

I know that my blessings are on the way. I will continue to hold on to His unchanging hands. I know that my season is now and I am expecting a miracle.

* * *

Today is May 13th at 12:40pm. I was just thinking about my daughter and grandchildren. I went back home for Mother's Day to spend some time with them. I really enjoyed them and they were glad to see me and that made my day. My daughter, granddaughter, and I are getting along much better. I have been praying to God to put us back together again as a family and it happened, so I know firsthand that prayer changes things.

* * *

Today is June 6, 2014 at 1:45pm and I thank God for another day. It has been a tiresome day trying to hold down two jobs. My body is tired and I am just trying to make ends meet. There are days that I get frustrated and feel like giving up, but I know that I can't do that. There are days I feel like grabbing a cold beer and saying "forget it" and I know I cannot do that either because I use to be a drug addict and an alcoholic and one little slip is all it takes.

I have now been clean for seven years, nine months and 6 days. I thank God because if it was not for Him and His grace and mercy I would not be alive today.

As I continue to strive to be a better Christian and be more Christ-like the Devil keeps throwing things at me. I know that it is only a test and truthfully, sometimes I let it get the best of me. I know I have to hold on because there is a light at the end of the tunnel.

Also while striving to be a better Christian I try to read my bible every day and stay focus on God, but I do get distracted every now and then. However, I know I have to keep Him first in my life and if I do not I will not make it.

The word: Jeremiah 29:11, God says "For I know the plans I have for your life".

God had put some powerful people in my life to help me follow Him. The Devil tries to get me all confused thinking about past situations. He keeps telling me that I will never amount to nothing, the Devil is a liar and the truth is not in Him. My everyday walk is continuing to tell me that "you can do this". I just got to put more faith in God and know that He will not let me fail and if I fall He will pick me up again. This is what makes me stronger and stronger as I continue to strive to be a better Christian.

CHAPTER 15

Kingdom Men

Today is Thursday, July 17, 2014 and the day is going pretty good for me. At church, the men hosting the bible study series was on "Kingdom Men" and it has been great.

I've learned that in order to be a Kingdom Man you need to change the things that you do in your life. Firstly, your attitude, then the way you live, and then the way you act and treat one another.

I have a heart of gold. I enjoy helping others. I want to be the man God created me to be. I want to serve Him with my whole heart. In addition, when He calls me home, I want to be ready to meet my maker. We all are put here on earth for a purpose and a reason. God has delivered me from alcohol and I want to work for Him.

I want to spread His word and I want to let people (young and old) know how God has changed my life, my actions, my appearance and my everything. If He can do it for me, then He can do it for you. If you want to me a Kingdom man you must live a righteous life.

CHAPTER 16

Birthday Travel

Today is the 23rd of July and I turned forty-nine today. Thank you God because if Satan had His way, I should've been dead a long time ago. Thanks be to God for His grace and mercy because if it was not for Him I would not be alive today to share my testimonies.

Today is the day I arrive at the airport 5:05am. I got my luggage and checked on my ticket and flight. The time came to board the plan; as I sat in my seat, I was so nervous; I made the best of it. We all sat there preparing for takeoff and as the plane went down the runway, we picked up speed, it was thrilling and scary. We went higher and higher. The pilot came on to make announcements about the temperature and our arrival time, the altitude was 22,000ft and climbing. I was just saying to myself, I do not want to hear any of this. I just want to get to my destination safely.

We made it to Atlanta, and then I had to change flights for Bridgeport, Connecticut. Once again back on the plane, I was a whole lot calmer. We flew for about 2 hours and 20 minutes. It was a nice trip. My brother-in-law picked me up and we stop by hospice to see my sister. The reason I flew up here is that I knew she would be glad to see me and I was glad to see her. I thank God that she was still here. My sister asked the doctor how her chances looked. And he told us that there is nothing else that they can do and we just have to wait and let nature take its course. I went to see her every day that I was there. I kept on praying and praying.

I know that prayer changes things. I will continue to trust God and whatever His will is then I have to still give Him praise. He knows what my sister needs. He is God all by himself. I am trying to enjoy myself but my sister is always on my mind. I went to my brother's church today and I really enjoyed the service. The speaker today preached on "You Can't Limit God". So that also brought confirmation on when the lady was in debt and when God told her to get all the empty barrows she could find. God begin to fill that up with oil. My pastor in Charleston spoke on the same thing about a month ago. If you heard it once, you will hear it again. God is good all the time.

* * *

Today is Monday, July 28, 2014, I got to the airport to catch my flight back, and I was not able to get on. I had to purchase my ticket and that line was so long. I got a discount on a buddy pass so I was on standby. Three flights had left and I was not able to get on either one. I was so ready to get to my destination; and I have to work later today. I am trusting that God will get me home today safe and sound. I know that the Devil is so ignorant and He is always trying to get someone distracted, but I know that I am going to get home soon. I do not want to lose my job because I have bills to pay and to keep up with. You know when you try to do good, stay in the will and walk with God; it looks like there are all kinds of things that will get in the way and try to hinder you. I am going to keep on holding on to God's unchanging hands because I know that He is able and I know God has no limits on what He is able to do. Remember that God is going to do just what He said He is going to do because He is a God that does not lie.

***Michael's Tip* #20**: Continue to put your whole heart into it and really trust in His holy word. I know that it is going to get rough sometimes and it is going to get trying and tempting, just know that God is in charge. He created the heavens and earth. Have you ever wanted something so bad and worked to serve the Lord with everything you have and it seems like you are not getting what you think or doing what you supposed to be doing? I know I do. I catch myself thinking that way. That is when I start praising and worshipping God more.

I am attending church regularly and I am paying my tithes. God has taken the alcohol and drug taste from me. I am doing pretty good. God said to wait on Him and lean not on your own understanding. There is a God, a healing God, an awesome God and an almighty God. It is hard being a Christian, it is a challenge and at the end, glory hallelujah, oh what a time. Oh what a time we will have in Jesus name.

CHAPTER 17

Getting ready for heaven

Today is August the 8th and my sister funeral is tomorrow August 9th and I am not looking forward to this day. I know it is here and I feel like I am in a dream and it is still hard to believe that she is gone. I just need to let God do what He has to do. I am just trying to get myself ready for heaven.

The Wednesday night service I attend at my church is in North Charleston and the minister preached on "If you miss Heaven You Are Going to Hell". I agree with that one. There is only two places you can go and that is heaven or hell and it is our choice.

I choose heaven any day. I look back on my life and I see where God has brought me from "alive". Of all the stupid and dangerous predicaments that I put myself in; I basically chose hell but right here on earth. Remember the choice is yours to make. Make sure it is the right one because if not, you are going to end up somewhere you do not want to be; perhaps prison or worst in your grave.

I prefer neither and I advise you to do the right thing. I am speaking especially to the younger generation. Another thing, please choose your friends carefully. Most of the time they are not really your true friends like God, either they are looking for something or they are trying to hinder you from achieving something you want. Live your life for

God; He has your best interest at heart and believe me there is no better place to be than to serve the Almighty God our savior.

* * *

It's September 9th and it has been **eight years and 9 days since I've been clean and sober**. I owe it all to God and while I was inconsiderate back in May to July I made God a promise, that if He would get me out of some trouble, I will serve Him. He has done that so I had to put that bottle and crack down; sniffing coke and all the other crazy things that I was doing. He delivered me from behind the jailhouse walls.

* * *

Today is September 23, 2014 and I am thinking about all I have been through; how God brought me through all my situations. I just want God to take me in His arms and hold me; to continue to change me from the inside out. I also want Him to change my attitude and the way I think. I have asked Him to give me a peace of mind and I want to be a better Christian. I want to have a big impact on other people lives and to let people know that God is real and he hears your cries for help and I am getting ready for heaven.

CHAPTER 18

The devil is busy

Today is October 7, 2014 and it's 10:41pm. I am at work and the Devil is trying to attack me with health issues again. I felt like leaving but stayed and noonday prayer was off the chain. God is really using Rev. Miller. This mighty woman of God is teaching us to serve God and to live a much better life. A lot of us still hold people's past against them. To them it does not matter how much you have changed your life as far as they are concerned you will still always be a bad apple to some.

Another young lady at noon day prayer by the name of Ms. Bernadette who is one amazing woman, stated that it doesn't matter what the Devil tries to throw at her, it doesn't bother her and her faith is mighty strong. This lady knows what the Lord has done for her personally and she loves Him dearly. She is one of the nicest women I have ever met.

As of today, Tuesday October 7, 2014, **I am eight years, one month and 7 days clean and sober.** If it had not been for the Lord, I would not be here. I know for myself, it does not matter what I go through, God is going to bring me out. I am still breathing, walking and talking after everything. It was not anybody else but, the Lord. I lost one of my sister's on July 11th of 2013 and lost another sister on July 30th in 2014. This really hurt me because it all happened so fast and it is still hurting. I encourage you to love your family every day, as if it was your last day on earth, because you do not know when it is your time to be called in the number that God has assigned to each of us.

Sometimes I ask God why I go through these trials and tribulations. Someone once told me that I am not supposed to question God, but I think God does not mind when we have issues and the devil is toying with us. I think He wants us to know why we go through certain things. Then we can change whatever we are doing wrong. It is still hard to picture my sisters gone and sometimes I do not want to accept that they are no longer here with me. I miss my sisters so, so much. It is truly hard when you lose a love one. I loved my sisters because they were always there for me when I needed to talk. She always told me how proud she was of me and for turning my life around; that really made me feel good that she cared so much about her little brother. She will always have a special place in my heart. I was proud of myself because I thought I would drink myself to death, glory be to God; if it had not been for Him, I don't know where I would be.

Since I have been walking with God, my life has really changed. I no longer do the things I use to do or hang around the folks I use to. Yes, a lot of them believe that I think that I am better than them but, that's not true. I just changed my life style of living. Some of these people are still in recovery from alcohol and drugs. I still have to be careful of the temptations because I do not want to go back to that kind of life because the devil is busy and always looking to get us trapped.

If you ever think about taking that first drink and that first puff of a cigarette, joint or sniff of cocaine, hit of crack cocaine, acid, shot of meth or heroin DO NOT DO IT. The road is definitely not fun or easy. When you are out there getting into trouble and doing drugs and acting stupid, you are not only hurting yourself, it hurts your family and friends too. Cocaine is a very powerful drug to overcome so do not get started and that way you will not get hooked on it.

* * *

Today has been a very trying day and the Devil is always trying to use a family member of mine to make me go back to the way I use to be. Since I changed my life I had family members that went behind my back and talk about me. Many of them sat in my presence, smiled in my face and acted as if everything was alright.

The word: Psalms 1says, *"Blessed is the man who walks not in the counsel of ungodly, nor stands in the path of sinner, nor sits in the seat of the scornful; But his delight is in the law of the Lord, And in His law he meditate day and night".*

I want God to use me and I want to serve God and do His will and not mines. Everything that I accomplish I want God to get all of the glory and praise; if it was not for God I could not have done it. When you use drugs, it changes the way you think, act and it takes over your mind. If you are weak, it can ruin your life. It can even make you take everything from your family and friends.

As I think back over my experiences, some of the things that I went through, it haunts me, and it keeps me from going back and sometimes it helps me to make better choices in life. I know I have to keep on trusting in God and lean not on my own understanding. I am so bless to be alive today. I took life for granted, for too many years and it nearly cost me my freedom and my life. ***I am telling you that if you do not know God now is the time to get to know Him.*** The sins of this world has taken over and people have lost their natural born minds. There is so much killing, lying, stealing, cheating and so much more. Sometime in my conversation with others, the subject of drinking comes up then I begin to tell my story on how I use to be an alcoholic, drug addict (crack cocaine) and a liar. I am so glad that I do not look like what I have been through. I was tore up from the floor up and I still need **God** to fix me up some more. I want to serve Him with all my heart, strength and soul no matter what comes my way in life whether it is good or bad.

CHAPTER 19

Oh how My Mom Prayed for Me

I give God all the glory because He can make a way out of no way. **The word:** Philippians 4:13 reminds me that I can do all things through Christ who strengthens me. I thought about when I was doing meth and how I never got anything out of it. **NOW** when I see people who are hooked on it I think to myself that is one powerful drug because it will change your whole appearance. I am thanking God for everything that He has brought me through from alcohol, drugs, porno, partying and excessive lottery playing. Although every now and then I still play the lottery, I'm just praying that God will take that away from me completely too.

If I wasn't adopted by my mom; who knows where I would've end up. My mother kept me in church. Somewhere down the line though I strayed away. My mom died in 1993 and it has been 21 years now since her passing and still today it haunts me how rude and disrespectful I use to be to her.

I now know that it was not me but, the drugs and alcohol that had me so messed up. I am truly, very sorry for my disrespectfulness to her. I know now that she is smiling down at me and saying "my son has finally turned his life around". My God, how my mom use to pray for me. She used to tell me, "Michael I don't know if you are doing drugs or not, but if you are it's going to take your voice away". Every time

I use to smoke crack I would hardly talk or get the words out of my mouth, I would lie and say I was not using drugs, but she being my mom always knew.

I believe that if I did not start drinking then I would not have used drugs. The reason I said this is because when I drank it triggered my mind that I needed something stronger.

I use to smoke weed and I did not like the mood swings that came along with it. Most of the time it would leave me feeling paranoid. It made me think of things that happened a long time ago; drinking put me in the state of mind that I needed this, I needed that and now I know it was only a mind game.

But look at me now, God has turned all of this around for me so I'm giving him the glory and I know its because of my Mother's Prayer.

* * *

I am so, so blessed to be alive today. I use to drive home after a party of drinking and having a good time. I remember during the winter months and it was freezing cold; I had to ride down the road with the windows down, so that I would not pass out before I made it home because I was so high and drunk. When morning came, sometimes I would wake up in the car. I also remember I use to walk around looking like a bum because I just did not care about what I looked like. When I had no way to get around, I use to call my so call friends that did not have time for me if I did not have a few dollars to give them. It was worse when I had no money because they pretended not to know me, but look at me now. No more sleepless nights and no more fake friends.

* * *

Today is Wednesday morning 3:47am, October 22nd and I'm still at work; as I think back and I can remember when I was staying in Connecticut, my sister left us in the house and my brother had moved in with his girlfriend and my girlfriend and I was living together. There was another friend living there too. Me, my girlfriend, and my roommate use to get so high and somewhere down the line our water was shut off, then the lights, but it was so bad we didn't even care. So we continued to get high by burning candles so we could see. It was so bad that we did not have anything to eat. My friend went to the soup kitchen, but I was too embarrassed to go. There was plenty of nights that I went to bed hungry. I use to hustle selling things to get enough money to buy food and drugs. I did not know where the next meal was coming from; but God always kept food to eat even if it was only a little, which is why through it all I still have to give him the Glory.

CHAPTER 20

My Sobriety

The streets, drugs and alcohol almost destroyed my entire life because I wanted to do things my way. For twenty plus years, I smoked crack cocaine and was putting all that poison in my system. I am now 49 years old. **I have now been clean and sober for eight years, one month and 22 days.**. I know that I am blessed. I owe it all to the almighty God. However, I cannot lie, ever since I have been walking with God it seem like I have been tempted even more. There have been temptation after temptation and it has been rough because just to get away from daily stressors sometimes I have felt like giving up and going back to the drugs.

However, I am not going to do it because I promised God that I will win this race and that is what I am going to do without any doubt. I want to reap all the rewards HE has promise me and to see this book help many people. My sobriety is everything to me.

I never use to pay my tithes and offering in church, now I do and I love giving Him His off the top because it belongs to Him. I do not praise God like I should because I often think what people would think about me crying. I am praising Him more in thought because of where He has brought me from and all the trouble He has save me from and every bad situation that I have put myself in. I am glad that I serve the Lord and I am so glad that He changed my life; thank you God. Where would I be if it weren't for God on my side? I know that crack cocaine is a very powerful drug. If you are not hooked on it yet, please do not get started. If you are using drugs seek help and talk to somebody, because it will destroy you and take everything you have. It will destroy your home, your marriage, it will make you lose the will to live and to achieve your goals and accomplishments or any dreams you may have planned for your life. Remember that when you are getting yourself into all kinds of trouble, causing confusion, and hurting others, you are also hurting yourself, your family and the people that surround you. So choose the right people to hang around, make the right choice in life and not the wrong choice; if that first decision you make isn't the right one, it could cause you your freedom and/or your life.

I came up in church. I had an awesome mom who raised me. This woman took me in and adopted me when I was only a baby. She was there when I was drinking and running around acting crazy like an asshole, now I am all about serving the almighty God. I am not perfect and I ask God to fix me all the time. If He had done all this for me, then I know that He could do it for you. So why not give Him a try and you will see what He can do.

Michael's Tip #21: **I beg you to please trust God and see how amazed you will be. See how well your life will change.**

Every day I wake up, I bow to thank God for waking me up in my right mind and for my health and strength and most importantly allowing me to become sober. I need Him to keep me safe from this cold, cruel world that we live in today. Every day is a walking journey for me to defeat the enemy. And there are so many obstacles that comes up in my life that at times I get frustrated and I think about what God has brought me through and where I came from and that makes me want to strive that much harder to get to my destination and to where God wants to take me.

* * *

It has been two months and twenty days since my family and I laid my sister to rest, and it still hurts very, very much. It is hard for me to believe that she is gone. One day last week, I was going to call her on the phone and then I realized that she was gone. Mostly every time something happens, I get the finger pointed at me because of my past. It is always something and despite my sobriety, it is something else when you feel like you are not welcome by your own family. It hurts but, I am learning to block a lot of stuff out and that is why I pray to God to bless me with another job, first shift, a great pay. I heard a saying once "that family is the worst people to deal with" now I know what that means. Many people just need God in their lives. I try to stay focused on God every day because He is the only way that I am going to make it to heaven and get my blessing while I am still living. He is the only way to go. I am alcohol free just because of Him. I am definitely still alive because of His grace and mercy.

* * *

Today is Sunday, November 9th at 8pm and today was a good day. Church services today was off the chain. The pastor who brought the message spoke about people and how church people talk about everybody and try to get into everyone's business else except for their own self. It is a shame how we pretend to love the Lord and others; when it comes down to helping our Christian brothers and sisters that's when you will find out that is really in your corner. I want to serve God with all my heart, mind, soul and strength. I want people to see how God changed me into the real man that He has put on this earth to be. I am going to perform my duties as a Christian man. I am going to finish my journey as a child of God. I am going to walk along with God.

I will stay alcohol and drug free because it means so much to stay clear of the drugs and alcohol. My addiction almost took my life and freedom. I want to reach young and older men and women all over this world to tell them about the goodness of Jesus. I want their souls to be saved. I cannot stress enough to people that crack cocaine is a powerful drug and it is a drug that you should not take lightly. It is a hard addiction to beat. It will take over the mind. When I was out in the world drinking and smoking crack, I was gone out of my mind. I use to hear bells ringing in my head and sometimes everything would go black and I could not see for a few seconds. My heart use to beat at a faster speed. I was always paranoid and thinking that the police or someone was watching me. It made my eyes look big and bulged. It kept me up for days at a time. I was not eating like I was supposed to. When I was out there in the world, I lost weight. I was already small, but the crack just made me look smaller or anorexic. I stayed depressed and I thought about suicide daily.

My goal in life was not to live; but drink and get high. I tried acid, meth, weed, pills and crack. Crack cocaine was my choice of drug. I never knew that I was going to be an alcoholic and drug addict. You never know what life is going to throw at you. You have to keep yourself in a safe environment. Keep yourself prayed up; stay grounded in the word of God. You also need to keep your focus on God it is easy to get side tracked and tangled up with the wrong crowd. I have been there so I know. I went down the wrong road plenty of times. When I was trapped in the life of alcohol and drugs, I did things that I knew I would not have done if I were not drinking, sniffing or smoking crack cocaine. My addiction helped me forget about my problems temporarily. I no longer thought about the pain and hurt that I went through with my birth mom, who gave me away. After she gave me away, she had another child. I often thought why me; I did not do anything I was still a baby. I would drink and drink my problems away, and then came the drugs. I thought I was helping myself. I never knew who my real father was, but I had my foster father until he died in 1972. I now have my heavenly father who will never leave me or forsake me and has kept me sober and that is all that matters.

CHAPTER 21

Catching Hell

My day has been great but very interesting. A reverend at church said that when you first wake up in the morning the first thing you should do is tell God thank you, even before you put your feet on the floor. Even before, you check your messages on your phone. He hit it right on the head because that is exactly what I was doing. I would grab my phone first to see what kind of message I got overnight. Now that has changed, each morning I wake up I tell God thank you for letting me see another day. He did not have to wake me or my family up, but He did. He is the almighty God, why shouldn't I tell Him thank you and give him the praises He deserves. He told me that before; I know my God and He knows me. I just keep leaning on Him and I have to keep building up my trust. He is God of many blessings and many miracles that have my name on it and no one else can get it but me. When God bless me, I am going to let everybody know that it was the almighty God who came to my rescue and not man. You just cannot beat God's giving, no way.

I know that being a Christian is not easy and at times I do catch pure hell from the Devil who does not want me to do good. I know that **"No weapon formed against me shall prosper, and every tongue which rises against you in judgment you shall condemned." This is the heritage of the servants of the Lord, and their righteousness is of** me," Says the Lord: Isaiah 54:17.** It also says in Proverbs 1:7; "**The fear of the Lord is the beginning of knowledge, but fools despise wisdom and instruction**".

I have lost a lot of love ones that I loved so much. I know that as God gets ready for me He is going to call me on. I pray and hope that God grant me more life to see my beautiful grandchildren grow up to be young women and men. I have three beautiful granddaughters and one handsome grandson. I missed not seeing them on a frequent basis due to the relationship my daughter and I have. I am going to keep on praying because I know prayer changes things.

* * *

Today is Tuesday, November 11th and it's Veteran's Day. I know that there is a lot of homeless veterans and people that have no place to go or anything to eat. I pray all the time asking God to bless me so that I can bless other people. I want to be able to have a big building to shelter the homeless and to get them off the street. At least they will have food to eat and a warm place to lay their head. When I see situations like that, I know it is only the Devil that has them there. In addition, because I have been there I know that we all need help at some point and time.

We never know if we will fall down and need some help. I know that some people think that it cannot or will never happen to them. But believe me it can and I know because I've been down that road. I use to sleep in my mom's house with no lights or heat. It was very cold and then family members who believed that I did not need to live there because of my addiction problems took that away from me. I also use to stay in my brother's mobile home that he abandoned years ago and never returned to in our home town in Hartwell, Georgia. Which is a small noisy town where everybody was in your business. I also stayed there with no lights, running water or food. It was a nice place at one time; I guess with no one staying there it got ran down. I had nowhere to go and alcohol and drugs had taken over my life. I was struggling with my problems and I did not want to work. I just wanted to get high. I was just wasting my life away

* * *

Today I got up early to go search for a second job at the temporary agency. The one I went to did not look safe so I left them. As I walked away, my spirit told me to go to the star gospel mission. I once stayed there until I got myself back together. The guys who stayed there was from all different walks of life and we were all there to get our lives back together. Some made it out and did well and some did not. Pastor Christian was a caring person who was there when you needed to talk or had a problem that you were burden with. The fee to stay there was $90 and it was well worth it. We had a laundry room and we had a cook that knew how to cook. I enjoyed my stay there. Therefore, whatever your situation may be; put your trust in God, because He will bring you through if you just hold on to God's unchanging hands. There are days when I go through my trials and tribulations, that I feel all alone. Then I remember what Proverbs 3:12 says, **"For whom the Lord loves He corrects, Just as a father the son in whom he delights"**.

I noticed that strangers would treat you better than your own family. There are times when I want to go somewhere, where there is no family around. Sometimes it is better not even being around them because of the way they treat you. I have learned to wait on God to bless me with my own. I asked him to remove me from where I am not welcome. As you get older, you realized that some of the things that you put yourself through was not the right choice and it caused you to fall off and get into trouble and that is when I think most of the things that my mom told me not to do. I was hardheaded and just wanted to be grown. I wish I had listened especially when I got into trouble and feeling guilty, it was always too late. My mom was always right when she told me things; I thought I knew more than she did. The Devil really had me fooled plenty of time. Many times I knew the things that I was doing wasn't right, but I did them anyway. I know most of the time that I was high on drugs and alcohol; I was in another world. I did not understand my life or situation and my actions for the things that I was doing. My life as an alcoholic and drug addict was frightening and confusing with all the pain and hurt I carried around with me. I do not worry about the past anymore because it was just holding me back. I am just taking it one day at a time with God. He has really changed my life for the better. I really want to forget about all the bad things that has happened in my life from the past. I want to really be happy, smiling and keeping it moving. I want it to really work with my daughter and I so I can have my grandchildren in my life. I just want to do God's will that He has for my life and to let myself grow to be a true man of God. I have to continue to build my faith up and to let go of a whole lot of stuff that happened in my life from the past. I let go and then I get unfocused because of the bill collectors, people especially family members that talk about me or lie on my name and other things that try to keep me confused. I continue to ask God to fix me because I was tore up and I need Him to lean on and to continue to teach and guide me through all the bad spirits that try to linger in my spirit.

CHAPTER 22

Blessed to be in the Number

Today is Sunday, November 16th another day that God has allowed me to see; thank you God. I know that someone did not wake up this morning, so I am blessed to be in the number one more day. We all want God to bless us no matter what kind of way we are living and doing what we know that is not right. I said we, but I am going to used myself.

God continues to work on me because I need to be fully delivered from all the mess. I still have lusting problems; I do not like to be alone. I am still single and I just keep asking God to keep me strong so I am going to wait on Him. I do not want just a woman who is just in it for what she can get; I want someone who is strong and who can help me build my life.

The scripture says "I had fainted unless I had believe to see his goodness of the Lord in the land of the living wait on the Lord and be of good courage, and He shall strengthen thine heart, wait I say on the Lord".

It is said that we all have a purpose in life and back when I was out in the world doing everything I wanted to do and go wherever I want to go. I had it twisted and I did not know whether I was coming or going. I wanted to do better and I wanted to change, but my addiction was stronger than I was. It had me thinking that I needed it and really, it was controlling my mind. I couldn't grasp myself to see that and plus at that time I thought that I was healing my pain and hurt that I was carrying around with me on a daily basis and before I knew it years had gone by and I was still dwelling on the past.

Dwelling on the past was just holding me back from where God wants me to be and what He wants for me to do. I was not ready and I was not right in God's eyes. I never thought that I would commit a crime that will label me as a felon. I never thought that I would be an alcoholic or drug dealer either. I drank lots of alcohol and smoked a lot of crack cocaine and I am not ashamed to tell someone that now because I want to prevent someone else from going down the same path that I did. Maybe I can have an impact on their lives. If they are on that path and are willing to change, then I know that God can heal and help them as He has done for me.

I use to think that once you have a felony on your record it is hard to get a job and sometimes it is. However, I have a felony on my record, God still blessed me with a job, and I owe it all to HIM. You know how it goes; people say that you need to know somebody that is willing to help you in order to get a job after you get a record. And I knew somebody and I know someone greater, his name is Jesus. He will put somebody in your life and make him or her flip the script. He will do it and He will blow your socks off on how he does it.

I have lost many of my love ones and some are still hard to deal with. I constantly ask God to make me stronger because it is very hard for me to deal with the passing of love ones. I think about how many times

God has spared my life because of my stupidity. My alcohol and drug addictions was terrifying back then and now that I'm clean and sober it is more terrifying when I think about how horrible the situation was that I put myself in and God took me out of them all. I was just living and not caring about my life or what happens to me; I made it with God's help. Although I am still struggling, I am working two jobs trying to get myself back on track. I still battle with bad thoughts that still pops in my mind. I know where I have been and there is no way that I will go back down that lonely, dark path again…Never.

I do not mind struggling until God says it is my season to be blessed. I am going to ride it out until God gives me favor. I know God has a blessing with my name on it and when God blesses me with it, no man can ever take it away. The power of God rules the Heavens and Earth, thank God. If it was in my hands, this world would be messed up even more.

I love living alcohol and drug free. I no longer worry about being pulled over for drunk driving or drug possession. I no longer walk around as if I am sick or looking strung out. I just have a peace of mind and it was definitely something that I really needed. I did not know how to be responsible. I was just living dangerously, now my alcohol and drug day are finally behind me. I have my mind set now to achieving things in life, like getting a good paying job, get my GED (I walked out of class and school in the 11th grade and I never went back). I also will like my own pressure washing and detailing business. I want to help put my grandchildren through college. I want to be there for my babies when they want or need something and most of all I want to get closer to God. I want to love everybody in spite of how they treat me. I want to be a blessing to others and I want to help people in need and continued to be blessed in the number.

CHAPTER 23

Giving Thanks

Today is November 27, 2014 and it is Thanksgiving Day. I just want to take time out just to day thank you God for waking me up this morning in my right mind. I thank God for giving me a roof over my head. I thank God for giving me food to eat. I also thank God for putting clothes on my back and for giving me life. I thank Him for my mind, hands, feet, arms, legs and/or sparing my life repeatedly. I want to thank God for saving me from a life of alcohol and drugs. I thank God for my family that loves me for me. I thank God for my beautiful daughter and grandchildren. I thank God for saving me and making me into the man I am today. I thank God for my health and strength. I Thank God for everything that He has brought me through.

* * *

It has been almost four months since I lost my sister and my heart is still heavy with pain that I am still carrying around and it still does not seem real. My sister was always there for me, for a lot of things and I Thank God for the time she was here with me. That is one of the reason I miss her so. She was an amazing woman. She will help anybody no matter what. She had a great heart and she was a very good cook. She could make a mean pan of lasagna. When I was out in the street doing badly and I wanted to get away, she opened her home to me and I stayed with her. She did so much for me. She is gone, but never forgotten by me. She was my big sister and always will be. My nickname is "Little Mike" and she was the only one that still called me by that name. There are days that I pick up my phone to call her and it comes back to me that she is now gone, but I give Thanks anyway.

None of us knows the time or the hour when God is calling on someone in my family or your family.

Michael's Tip #22: Get your life right with God before it is too late.

My foster mom fostered 21 kids in her home. She delivered over two thousand babies and she adopted four kids. It is a blessing for all the people lives, especially mines, and if it was not for her, I do not know where I would have end up. I thank God for putting her where she needed to be to raise me.

I still struggle some from time to time but I know that it is not going to be this way forever, with God by my side. It is just not my season yet, but I know it is on the way. I am getting ready for my blessing and I know that God has one with my name on it. Glory be to God, this is the day that the Lord has made so I am going to be glad in it. He has made me glad (smiling).

As the days go by, I am still asking God to do some things in my life. I am looking forward to it and every day I wonder if it is going to be that day. I know that God does things on his time and not mines; this is why I continue to hold on and pray. I know God wants me to be happy, stress free, worry free and so much more that God has prepared for me. I know the life that He wants me to live and I am a work in progress. I do need His help every single day because sometimes I think I am going to lose it. I thank God for His grace and mercy that I am still in the mist of this crazy mix up world that we live in. We all just need to come together and pray. I pray and pray until something happens. Prayer does change things. We need to pray for someone other than ourselves. Pray for the homeless you see walking, sitting or lying on the ground/sidewalk with nowhere to go. This could be you or one of your family members one day. I was once that person. I had nowhere to go and nothing to eat and I Thank God for bringing me through.

There was a young lady that I use to get high with; she used to go to the soup kitchen to get us something to eat. I was too ashamed to go there, but I was not too ashamed to go to the package store to get a 12 pack or a bottle of Seagram's Gin or whatever else I wanted. I was not afraid to spend my last five or ten dollars with the drug man either, but thank God I'm not there anymore either.

I remember when my mom use to take me and my adopted brother to church on Sunday and after Sunday service we would stop at everybody's house it seems like. In this day in age people don't do that kind of stuff anymore. Now people do not have time for you or anyone else and even themselves sometimes for that matter. It seems like all we want to do these days is to talk about each other and it really a shame we just cannot get along because we all need each other.

* * *

Good morning, it is December 26, 2014, the day after Christmas and I thank God for letting me see another day. My daughter was explaining to her kids, that it is not all about the presents and it is about the birth of Jesus Christ, the one who died for us on Calvary cross. I use to take it for granted; God choose me for, for goodness sake.

I did not make it home to spend Christmas with my daughter and grandchildren because I was down with the flu. I am in my grandchildren's life. Not like I want to be, but I am waiting on God to change that too. I want to be a big impact on their lives. To teach them to do the right things in life and know how to treat people, have respect for others and themselves. I want them to learn how to be independent, to succeed and get them motivated to achieve their goals in life. I want my babies to come up alcohol and drug free and to have love in their hearts. I also want them to take control of their lives at an early age; still enjoying being a kid while they are growing up.

*　*　*

It is now 12:36am, December 30th 2014, one more day before the beginning of a new year. On today's job schedule me and the other guys I work with wasn't scheduled for any work for the next few days. I was looking forward to working, to make ends meet. I left the job and I am thinking about going to noonday prayer. I have not been in a while. I decided to go.

Noonday prayer was off the chain and I am very Thankful for this opportunity. Rev. Miller is the one who is in charge of giving God's word. She is a serious real woman of God and a friend. She is a very gifted and powerful woman of God. The word for today was "New Beginnings". She said "whatever you don't get in 2014, it's done; whatever is going on in 2014 and it's not of God, let it go".

CHAPTER 24

Another New Year

In 2015 and I am asking God to do some new and improved things in my life. I asked God to remove all the junk that I am carrying around like my attitude. I have not fully let go. I am going to surrender all myself to God. I want all of Him. I want to stay more in His word and for Him to teach me how to become a better Christian, father and grandfather. I want to be a blessing to others. I want Him to send me a soulmate and that we love each other until death do us part. I want to go around spreading the gospel of Jesus Christ. I want to be in a position where I will tell people how He saved me from destruction, alcohol and drugs.

* * *

Today is January 1, 2015. Thank God for allowing me to make it through 2014. It was a struggle but my God brought me through it safe and sound. I want to say for the ones that didn't make it to see 2015, may your family be blessed in every way; that their family member is rejoicing in Heaven with the Lord. I want 2015 to be fruitful for my health and finances.

I want to walk in prosperity with Jesus and to keep my mind clear. I want to stay in God's favor, to continue to listen to His holy word more and more. I want to reach my goals and dreams that I have for myself. I want to go places that I thought I never imagined I could ever go. I want to do all the things that I thought I could never do because of my choices and drug addiction. I want to go all the way with God and to give Him all the praises that He truly deserves. I asked God to continue to show me mercy, grace and favor in my life. I want to walk boldly and be faithful in God. I want to listen more when God speaks and not quick to run off at the mouth. I want to learn how to watch out for people who are not real and do not have my best interest at heart. I want God to give me endurance to run this race.

In 2015, I am going to press my way to the top. I am going to love God to the fullest. I will not let my fear of what other people think of me when I am praising Him. I want to praise and glorify God with open arms. I want to get my blessings because I need and want everything that God has for me. I want these things to be released on me from the crown of my head to the sole of my feet. I want everything God has for me and then some; thank you Jesus.

* * *

As I think back when I use to drink and smoke crack cocaine, what a fool I was. I had a serious addiction and I was denying it. I denied my problems for many, many years and it got worse. I struggled through life with my addiction and I have been through things. I just want to share some of my past life experiences with you. I let my addiction get the best of me. My mind was in that stage of taking my own life. I knew that deep down inside it was not right; the alcohol and drugs had taken a toll on my mind. I was just living from day to day. I was in a deep depression state. I was not happy; I was lost. I felt myself falling and I could not stop it; but God could. On this 3rd day of January 2015, I am **eight years and 4 months clean and sober**. I had nothing to do with this, it was all GOD. It was His grace and mercy that save me from destruction and Hell; thank you Jesus.

CHAPTER 25

He showed up

The bible speaks and teaches me all kinds of wonderful works to the keys of my future; since I am human I tend to stray off into the world and the world is no good for me. I still struggle through life as I still listen to man and living off the world and how it is now. I want to rephrase this to say that people in the world are sometimes messed up and confused.

I see that some people who are murdering each other like it's a hobby and others are going into the schools and colleges with weapons and killing innocent people but that just means God hasn't shown up for them yet. I sometimes get so angry and frustrated when I see these kinds of things going on in the world. It is a shame and I am so grateful that God showed up in my life when he did because I wouldn't have made it without Him.

His grace and mercy saved me from a whole lot of destruction that was erupting in my life. I can tell you that God may not come when you want Him; but He is always on time. God forever seems to amaze me by what and how He does things.

God gave me the power to pray for myself and I am always asking other people to pray for me. There is nothing wrong with that, **Michael's Tip #23**: Be careful who you ask to pray for you because they may not have your best interest at heart. It is always better to ask God for healing or for whatever you need. I am asking God for some new things and to work some things out in my life as I said before. I have learn how to lean on Him instead of my own understanding. I want more and better things in my life.

I want to serve Him more and I want to bless Him with my tithes and offerings. I want to bless others. Once God showed up for me I learned that pride will get you nothing, but left out. It will harm you. It could leave you hungry. I have also learned that everybody needs somebody to help them in a time of need. My pride was not the only thing that was holding me back; I know how people are, either they do not have it at the time you need the help and some really do. Then there are some who will do it as a loan. Then they will go around telling everyone you do not want to know about your business. Then these same people will say to you "why you didn't ask me, I would have given it to you". I have learned that people will talk about you anyway. I have learned how to lean on God more and more every day.

I can't think of anyone who can bless, love and treat you like my Lord and Savior Jesus Christ. It is better to put your trust in God because He has all power. He is our provider. He is our Rock in a weary land. He can do what no other can do. I have been asking God to open doors for me, let people know how He has come into my life and turned my life around; from being alcoholic and drug addict. He showed me that there is a better way to live life.

In 2007 and 2008, when I was a resident at the Star-Gospel Mission for men, a place that help men get their lives back on track. I met Pastor Christian who was in charge of the program. He was a very nice person and he always had time for you, whether someone was going through an issue or if you just need to talk to someone at that time. One day when I was out looking for a second job and I stopped by the Mission to see how he was doing. He took the time to show me around the Mission. He asked how everything was and I told him. I told him that I was still clean and sober. He said he was very proud of me. He asked me to speak to a few churches to tell the story about my drug and alcohol addiction; most importantly to tell the people how God showed up and has changed my life and I did.

I spoke about what I went through and told them that it was nobody, but God. The first step is wanting to change your life and to want more for yourself. I know that I am going to prosper in life because God said **"But seek first the kingdom of God and His righteousness, and all these things shall be added to you"**. It also says **"For I know the thoughts that I think toward you, says the Lord, thoughts of peace and not of evil, to give you a future and a hope"** Now, if God has plans and He knows the plans, He has for me and I do His will; I will prosper in life. I have to do what I have to do to get what God has for me. I am going to pray and pray. I am going to serve and serve my God with my whole heart. The more I strive to do better and better the Devil try to throw stumbling blocks in my way; God has always and He will always bring me through, no matter what comes across my path. This is the kind of God I love to serve. There is no one that I can really trust, but God. My pastor have been preaching on prayer and lately that has been going around everybody is talking about prayer. Prayer changes things and the way this world is going we are going to need all the prayers we can get.

* * *

This is a new year and I have a new and improved attitude this year. I want God to transform my mind into positive thinking. I am going to stop worrying about the things that I cannot change and focus on the things that I can. I like telling people of the world, that no matter what you are going through it is only temporary. I want them to know that if you put God in your situation it is bound to change and only if you have faith in God that He can bring you through anything. I am a living, walking testimony that He can do it. I want to touch as many lives as I can because God really has fixed me up and turned me around for the best. I really want to be the kingdom man that I know I can be. I want to be successful in everything I do. I want my walk to line up with God. I want to be obedient to His word and to learn more about Him. I want to study more. I want to praise and worship Him with my entire being no matter what type of day that I am having because at the end of the day I am smiling again. I know that God will bring you through once again.

* * *

Today is Friday, January 16, 2015 and I am coming to the end of this journey. If you have read my self talks and journal entries, just know that God has your best interest at heart and He can make a way out of no way. I encourage you to keep on believing and trusting in His word.

Everything I spoke about in this book is real. There are no games. It happened to me and there is more. I just wanted to share some of my testimonies with you that God has delivered me from. Nobody, but God almighty. I encourage each of you to search your heart and see where you line up with God. Are you really true to God? Do you really love others the way you say you do? Remember that God knows everything about us even the things we don't know about ourselves. I know I don't read His word on daily basis; I am trying to do better.

Michaels tip #24: I recommend that you read His word on a daily basis.

I have learned to trust God and take Him at His word. I am beginning to hunger and thirst for His word every day. To grow spiritually with God, we need His word. I know if I keep on praying about it and speaking it into the atmosphere, it will come to past. Be encouraged my sisters and brothers. I hope that my stories and testimonies have changed, helped, or encourage someone along the way. There is more to come until then please continue to stay prayed up and blessed in the name of Jesus, Amen.

Michael Burton

Notes

Notes

Notes

Notes

Notes

Notes

Notes

Notes

Notes

Contact Info

MichaelBurton44@gmail.com

Facebook/Michael Burton

Order online at amazon.com and all other online distributors

Coming Soon!!!!

The Day After:

The Struggle is Over…My time to Shine

Interested in Writing and or Publishing a BOOK???

Visit: www.A2ZBooksPublishing.com

www.ingramcontent.com/pod-product-compliance
Lightning Source LLC
Chambersburg PA
CBHW021155080526
44588CB00008B/353